T0057556

Mouth Filled with Night

SERIES EDITORS

John Alba Cutler

Reginald Gibbons

Susannah Young-ah Gottlieb

John Keene

Ed Roberson

Mouth Filled with Night

Poems

Rodney Gomez

NORTHWESTERN UNIVERSITY PRESS

EVANSTON, ILLINOIS

Northwestern University Press
www.nupress.northwestern.edu

Northwestern University Poetry and Poetics Colloquium
www.poetry.northwestern.edu

Printed in the United States of America

10   9   8   7   6   5   4   3   2   1

Library of Congress Cataloging-in-Publication Data
Gomez, Rodney, author.
  [Poems. Selections]
  Mouth filled with night : poems / Rodney Gomez.
    pages cm. — (Drinking gourd chapbook poetry prize)
  ISBN 978-0-8101-2977-1 (pbk. : alk. paper)
  1. Mexican Americans—Ethnic identity—Poetry. I. Title. II. Series:
Drinking gourd chapbook poetry prize.
PS3607.O496A6 2014
811.6—dc23

                                                      2013039157

♾ The paper used in this publication meets the minimum requirements
    of the American National Standard for Information Sciences—
Permanence of Paper for Printed Library Materials, ANSI Z39.48-1992.

Contents

Acknowledgments

I owe my gratitude to the editors of the following journals and anthologies where some of these poems originally appeared:

Backbone: "The Method"

Bayou: "Escutcheon for Pochos"

Borderlands: Texas Poetry Review: "Río Bravo"

BorderSenses: "A Farmer, a Chain"

Denver Quarterly: "Milpa Verde"

Devil's Lake: "Farmworker as Existential Quantifier"

A Face to Meet the Faces: An Anthology of Contemporary Persona Poetry: "Baedeker for a Life Cut with Danger"

Fourteen Hills: "La Sirena"

Harpur Palate: "What Happened to Fire"

Nimrod: "Speaking River"

Ostrich Review: "Feast Day"

The Pinch: "Riot"

RHINO: "Cornelio Smith" and "Drag Racer"

Salt Hill: "Mesquite Virgin" and "The Hand"

Vision/Verse: "Grackle"

Foreword

One of the beautiful poems from this first chapbook by Rodney
Gomez begins, "Every Mexican boy wants a drag racer. A warhead to
mount, tear / ribbons from downtown's irregular heart. . . ." In "Drag
Racer," a father questions "what every boy needs to become a man" and
what he has given his son. The imagery is drawn from Mesoamerican
mythology, mainly Aztec. The wings in the shape of his own hands
that the father makes for the boy recall those of the Earth Mother,
Coatlicue, whose hands were torn off by a daughter, Coyolxauhqui,
who incited her hundreds of siblings to rebel against their mother and
kill her. Huitzilopochtli ("Hummingbird of the South"), born fully
grown and armed at the instant of his mother's death, kills most of the
children and throws his rebellious sister down the mountain.

The father in "Drag Racer," who has made his son a pair of black
wings, asks specifically if a boy needs the forces of light or those of dark
to become a man. With no regard it seems for a father's wishes, the son
at the end of the poem has all the qualities of Xochipilli, "The Prince
of Flowers," the god of agriculture, music, song and poetry, dance,
weaving, and embroidery. He is the twin of Xochiquetzal, "Precious
Flower." The twins share the domain of fertility, but she represents
female sexuality, young mothers, and childbirth, while he represents
the sexualized male, including homosexuals and male prostitutes. As
the patrons of psychoactive agents, including mescalin, psilocybin, and
tobacco, the twins are raw human desire and pleasure raised to the level
of the spiritual. The two sometimes turn themselves into one another.
All the imagery—twins, sibling rivalry, dismemberment, sacrifice, and
redemption—appear in "Drag Racer" in a deeply respectful reworking
of Mesoamerican mythology.

The Spanish word for butterfly, *mariposa,* is Mexican and Chicano
slang for a gay man, so the point at which the boy becomes Xochipilli
is also the point at which the father recognizes his son's sexuality.

The last two lines of this poem are jaw-droppingly beautiful in the resolution they provide and the wisdom that they leave to the father, who watches his son weave night into a corsage.

I have gone into this poem in detail (by no means complete) to prepare the reader for the brilliant cultural exchange accomplished throughout this book via the imagery and mythology underlying these poems. Check out "La Sirena." Rodney Gomez, a welcome new poet, at least on the Eastern landscape. Send more in this direction.

The Hand

Midnight some time ago, I severed my hand & let it loose in the sugar cane fields outside my home. The next morning, being so drenched with want, I remembered how much a good hand is worth & went to find it. It was panting at a nearby well, next to a neat row of baskets filled with cane. Thinking it would easily reattach, I pressed it against my wrist—but strangely the hand didn't fit. It scuttled away & I followed, arriving at a city of cardboard in the brush where a highway of hands flowed, swollen & tired. My true hand was there, struggling to pull a time clock into a tattered shoebox. Under the lid was a bleeding pinpoint—glowing hot, too bright for my eyes—accepting into itself all our loveless works.

Río Bravo

I thrum a *bajo sexto* in the shallow Río Bravo.
A threnody, a war cry, bristle on the Río Bravo.

Walls serrate our womb, *pero no dividen a la gente.*
Eagle warrior corpses sail *el río sin candado.*

In riverless places I trace my veins in charcoal.
How'd I earn my brothers? Grifting on the *río malo.*

So many buried grave markers softened with lantana.
Blindfolded taggers aerosol the Río Bravo.

To ward off pellagra I built a launch out of tortillas.
Black-lunged *maquilas* fizzle at the *río dado.*

At night, on the hillsides, bridges frail as vertebrae.
Fishnets plied in broken bones wrestle with *el río.*

Vast sums move across, without ever showing a passport. *
Green shirts on Appaloosas pistol-whip the Río Bravo.

My mouth fills with night, the race memory of drowning.
With or without a fence, we missile through the Río Bravo.

* Eduardo Galeano

2

Milpa Verde

a gray lung used to glisten on the corner,
now's hard and pock-marked,
worships a scuffed curb clenched by a litter pile

  where they ran a laundry line of black trousers,
their flap a loud buzzing of wasps—a pleading language?—

cipher of crackle and jasmine-lavender stink
for the Laundromat's rusty womb:

domino-stacked block walls where the kingdom of cats rules
  who can flee flees, otherwise all stillborns

the bus stop littered with them—rhomboid shopping carts,
second helpings of Krylon:

a message on the window says *now more than ever
virtue matters,* a treatise written in dog blood beneath

  in one of the apartments a jobless teller
pours over *Luke* so as not to drag
the baby boy down the street into a headline:

  in the eyes of the mob pulling steel from concrete
a blemished copy of an actual kingdom

  a wet, glabrous nerve to pull up, beat black,
and torch with their devices

La Sirena

Civil Hispanic family, seated
around a table, eating
their store-bought mole.
Two children, male and female.
Two-parent home.
A beagle named Chiquita
festooned with pink ribbon.
Later, Mass at the Good Shepherd.
Much later, when the kids are asleep,
the wheelbarrow in a locked master bath,
an empty bottle of Presidente
lounging on custom tile.
A life-sized *lotería* card appears
at the table: La Sirena, most scandalous
of all square-cornered possibilities.
Lovely Mrs. Brown goes dumb,
then a little aroused with the size
of the interloper's breasts.
Mr. Brown is yoked by Catholic shame
and stifles the beagle's bark.
Only the children speak. One says
We have learned to escape
what is damning to us. The other
says her dreams are filled
with the fishy scent of the mermaid's
hair, the sea breath lingering over
the standard Mexican meal she
will fold in a towel
and flush down the guest room toilet.
After a while they continue to eat,
the mermaid speechless, drying out in
their unflinching habits.

At My Crutch's Funeral

My mother lets me in on a little secret: I'm not Mexican, but was born on Sirius C. The milkman brought you in a bottle, she says. You were scrunched up inside, swimming in the white heart. We tried to pull you out, but the bottle had an ostrich neck, so we broke it at the levee and let you wash away. You boiled the river dry. Nowadays one can walk from one side of the river to the other without ever feeling content.

Speaking River

hold your mouth shut
and you bring the river
into you

      odd that water would behave
      different than breath
           but in it—
                    gar, green bloom, cyclops—
      fugitives afraid to open throats
      to sun

I used to be you, declaiming

      use the jowls
      muscle my brown protest out

easier to expel
than imbibe
      saying without saying

I discovered the back of the teeth
muting the water's spine

      no allegiances
cutting the river root
with the tip of my folded tongue

Serape

(Adrian Esparza, *One and the Same,* 2005; serape, plastic trim, and nails)

When I turned eleven my mother gave me a serape smooth as axolotl skin. I wore it at dusk to draw offspring. I'd been told that if I buried it, a refugee would emerge. So I dug a grave between two *retamas.* I had never imagined a twin. But one morning, covered in mud, was a mirror of me at the front door. My mother wove him a coat to keep warm, and soon I never even existed. It's frightening to know how quickly a man without belief will disappear. All that was left was a desert, dense with thirst. This is what happens when you unravel a thing already unraveled—the body finds another body to cover the void.

What Happened to Fire

In the alley, a boy
would fly
a fish-shaped kite,

its nylon mouth
and feathery anus open
to air.

What held him there—
a single red fin

along a row of withering
gray spine, a flame
still flickering
in ash.

In those days
you expected fires,

wind that could calm
every thrumming nerve,

even among ruins,
even in the sky.

❧

By the berm
where someone was stabbed
in Garden Park,

every Sunday
a pair of black-bellied ducks
would beg for crumbs.

Although a mile north
they could have fattened

themselves on throwaways,
they remained.

They would waddle
in the shade
of a lime tree,

shape rinds into scythes
in their brown beaks
for the sparring.

⌁

What everyone remembered:
monkey bars, whirligig,
steel pigs stuck

with coils a super
clairvoyantly thought
to paint yellow

since what happened
only exists now
in newsprint.

We were offered a wisp
of devil there,
and when we said no
we were beaten until

all that remained
of our wormhole vision
was the blue cupola

of the movie
house, smoldering
in its own shadow.

The last thing I said
before going under
was a treatise on fire
so near my tongue.

Head of a Jewel Scarab

In an old photo of myself, I am wearing the head of a jewel scarab. I'd gone to my brother's wedding dressed as the rain god Tlaloc and pierced my septum with oleander. But the scarab I don't remember. I ask my *xolo, Do you remember this head? Yes,* he says. *That is the day you discovered survival.* A little after the wedding, I'd trapped a prayer to the god in my eye. To this day, everything I see is drowning.

Feast Day

At the field's navel,
      my father caulked
           around a smoldering
horse, head & mane
      hissing into obsidian
           blades, fasting
into lamplight.

He slowly peels corn
      like a wave machine.
           The cars loud as hooves.
The pit roars up like cotton,
      the odor of speed
           winding down
to death.

Nearby a clay womb
      we use to sleep
           & hide the bones,
brindle snaps, & clops.
      Another field fenced
           to keep wetbacks out.
When we lurch & run

our hands along the warmth
      of fire and neck,
           we almost forget

how metal scrapes
      against the tongue.

Cornelio Smith

For Rebeca

I fell in love with his girth. How he prowled the border wall and squawked whenever a wetback crossed. The farm's one glazed ornament. How could I resist? In a town like San Pedro you surrender yourself to strength—the bare plane of the engine, the barn's pitch and beams. You learn to worship the bark of a workshopped man. *Malinche,* my father yelled. *How can you love a chanticleer?* But I have a traitorous heart. Do you know, when they built the border wall they used Cornelio's beak? Every day he perched on a flatbed and called attention to the gaps. He was so good they airlifted him to Nogales for a week. When he left, I filled the dry river bed with tears. By the time he returned I had taken the wall as my throne. My gaze was magnificent, rummaging through shantytowns and patchwork cemeteries. I ran Cornelio off with a tire iron and rotisserie. Squatting in sunlight and pinpointing the refugees. Sopping up the love.

Farmworker as Existential Quantifier

For J.H.

That one waters
his mortgaged field

& becomes the water.
Another drinks the water

& dissolves into drills.
The quickest one coffins

into the trench with his wife.
They are there so long

a plow gives them last rites.
A child is born on that

hottest day in mid-strike.
He swallows the crop

& waddles away a god.
Without any fuel, workers

sell their own steam.
Their labors are packed

into a papoose & carried off.
One of them pours

the water onto his rags.
The rest of them catch

the wringed water
in their mouths.

Grackles

Every morning his daughter braids grackles into his hair. Works feather
& thrashing beak into the scour brush of his hair. For the rest of the
day he shrinks to a vole's rapid heart. Sweat pressed & forced into the
rapeseed of his heart. His plow, the head of his dented shovel, they
bray along with the beasts she meticulously grafts. Instead of naming
she kneads them into family with her own worker's hands. At the end
of the day what he pulls from a burlap sack staring after the gloaming:
tufts of grackle-shaped clouds, a grackle's stunted arpeggio, the after-
thought of flightlessness.

A Farmer, a Chain

(Luis Guerrero, *Lágrimas y sudor,* 1999; metal, steel, and fabric sculpture)

Do I anchor here, clanging
                    my lungs out, rueful
          as okra shivs, or go
unblind, roadblocks
          crumbling under my
                    questioning plow?
          I am impermeable and so continue
glistening, bandana signed
                    across my scalp and primed
          for any guerrilla attack of doubt.
Burdened by potbellied
                    obligation, I slink
          where the habit leads, palm
upon palm, burlapped
                    to a fallow. I used to be
          white once, and what marrow
will I scare off with my spade, and who
                    will follow me,
          and who will scrape
by, injuring their own critical apparatus,
                    hammock their life savings
          to sleep? I sleep
between two imperialist trees
                    across a thirsty lake,
          unconscious, unconscious.
No, I am not really
                    a farmer—call me spitshine,
          call me blunder and
perpetual yoke, but please
                    unburden me
          before I decide that this
sack of never, not now, is enough.

Escutcheon for Pochos

For Isaac

We rode slingshot with Tezcatlipoca. Devouring the sky's deterministic
bosom. Rain scherzos trailing us. Spitting *chapapote* from our
blackened mouths. Then the year we learned to scrape the talk box
from our lips. To inchworm cigarillos in yesterday's news, licking
seams with tongues that could metronome a phantom language.

A locksmith in maguey wig propped my skull on the bend sinister.
Pickled my exclamations in piquin to stutter out a proper welcome.
He called to the earth: *voy, vas, va.* To me: *fui, fuiste, fue.* Fishhooked
himself through my rogue throat. Language cop, come to pestel our
anarchy, filigree each stumble with the unforgiving gridwork of ball
cactus.

We slunk behind the scruff of a Plymouth, counting rear-enders in the
glare of a misspelled sign. Our cousins crouched on the awning on the
other side, blinking in and out of existence. Curling their neon fingers
towards us, slandering our *or* and *and*. The faster we ran, the faster their
voices nailed us. In the alley, bargain coffins inlaid with our molars.

Drag Racer

Every Mexican boy wants a drag racer. A warhead to mount, tear
ribbons from downtown's irregular heart. I made my boy a pair of
wings in the shape of my hands, knotted and black. The first thing
he did was fan himself on a hammock in the backyard. He slept for
days in a whirring cocoon, racing in his head. He flew water out to
the men building roads and the women pulling weeds in the prison
yard. He was drawn to future deserts. Finally he flew as I wanted him
to, out of bomb-shelled buildings. It was beautiful, the way his little
arms scattered sunlight over pockmarked asphalt. Erasing the blight,
imploding like a brown dwarf. One day I caught him at the tenement
rooftop in pumps and green mascara, the wings penciled into a prom
dress. So that was the white he wanted to wear, a mouth open with
light. Why I had always trusted the sky. What every boy needs to
become a man is night. Or so I thought, taking the black scroll from
my mouth. Watching him weave it into a corsage.

Riot

There was a riot in Bluetown
near a slab of balsa some said
held the Virgin of Guadalupe's face.
A native son of Puebla, praying at her
chancel, forgot to remove his plumage.
They thought he mistook her for Tonantzín.
There was something sinister
in the angle of his palms, though he accepted
ash like the rest, stayed for Rooster Mass.
Seizing his beads, they stopped
caring about pretense, hung
his phony corpse from the poplar tree
and hoped he'd snap just as he was:
skin pulled taut, face made up
in crude proxy of the true Virgin
whose face they adored.

Spine

Suppurating river,
who never mumbled
its declaration of peace,

what do you do with the bodies?

Is there beauty in concrete tongues?

When I was young they
scored the levee into a quiet
stream. Yet no one could speak
in cleaved speech.

Each shanty on Military Highway
handcuffed to a pinwheel
of factory smoke.

After the rabble rouser
refused to budge
she was buried alive
in the aspic to confirm
that a new body could be quickly
built by the agents' fingers.

Big rigs hauled the answer in.
Laid the red backbone along backyards.
Flytrap of hairstreaks and metalmarks.
Is this what it takes to blot out
fear?

When it didn't end you questioned me:
Would they fracture the spine
to raise a bridge?
Would they uproot the slats
to conceal the open wound?

A Theory of Fences

They told him to spread his arms
so they could chart a midnight
offensive on his naked back.

He cradled the raindrop march
of gun shots, then the wall folded
back on itself like a pitcher plant.

One of them carved the ideogram
for rain on the small of his back,
another the logic sign for union.

Another ran his hand along the spine
picturing fences and the way
he shivered in the dark as a child.

The Method

(José Balmes, *Realidad 10,* 1964; mixed media and collage on wood]

A coffin is a fine substitute for a gag.
So a voice grows larger in artifice: first son
pinned to a loom, spouse crumpled
into bullet wounds on the porch
where every dog barks night's slur.

The only ones speaking are bagged,
gurgling their telegraph through black
water like a liturgy.

Behind the yellow newsprint runs the law
of transitivity—one whimper bleeding
through obits, another taking the shape
of the voice to seal with gaffer tape.
There are other lives waiting to etch
themselves on live grenades.

The ash clouds drowned out by blood,
but murmur in the blood underneath,
and so remain as permanent as air, or walls,
or blood.

Is this real: as in, does this correspond
to something outside themselves,
or does it last, even when they don't think it?

They were asking too much about how the world
came to be so damp with blood, blood
stamped with peace, blood in the absolute
center of things, like a dipole, until the pistols,
sleek as Dobermans, uncovered them.

What was real against the wall, do they linger
once the last loud firecracker is spent?
Do they correspond to something outside themselves?

Prospective Titles for a Border Thesis

after Gloria Anzaldúa

Border as Blue Note Played Surreptitiously Under Every *Cumbia*

Border as Strychnine Substituted for Cal in a Tortilla Recipe

Border as Speedway Dimpled and Warped in the Manner of Braceros

Border as Black Butterfly Turned to Talc in Sun

Border as Vein Spilling Blood Blacker than Oil

Border as Glorious Coupling of Dysfunctional Pharynxes

Border as Womb Emptied of Night and Swallows

Mesquite Virgin

1

Does she notice the rain on the loose hem of her lip? How the dry dolls
sway & blur? Hands palmed together in a jewel case of warm velvet.
A slash & a wedge & a series of peelings—shawl's cascade, saint's cleft
chin. Her knee throbbing on the milk crate footstool. Sunk. Laboring.
What does she pray to? Or is she sleeping? Or has she realized the
absence?

2

If she yields to a dark room, does she yield to its tinging? To its slivers,
slashes, blood-letting? Does she contort herself in a shoebox? Fill herself
with gnashes? Foul-smelling? If the room grows big, does she grow big
with it? If it shrinks, does she carve her name with a miter saw? If the
room is empty, does she fill it?

3

To find the source of love, she digs until her cuticles bleed. Cuts open
the brains of mangosteens. Peels the paint & the ash remains. Axes
through wood & a void. Underneath the gray blocks—millipede eggs,
snail's operculum, bone hiding a further truth all the way down. In the
block upon block, a house, a bakery, a morgue. Behind the furniture,
the shadow of the furniture, & under the carpet the shadow of bare
feet, arguments. And in the nude, a scar of herself, or a vase that could
have been filled with water but chose to crack itself instead.

4

She lacks a sin to confess. But knowing everyone has something to
confess, she beats a friend unconscious with a mesquite branch, shoots
two rare blue cardinals. To herself: *& in your search, what is true?* She
replies: *a starving shoat eating rooster crops, smashed black widow bent as
a swastika, pink jelly of aborted possums.* Her arms, dark as bat wings,
enfold her carving body.

Grackle

If I had known that grackles dress their young
       I would have left out the bobbin.

A shadow sounds so lost in a basket,
       but there is always the full darkness of closed wings.
       La magia de la quiromancia.

My firstborn was a tessellation of bones
       and a grackle head. I cut my fingers on obituary
          newsprint. She cradled a nest to her head

and planted a stone. Struggled to name it—
       piedra, perdida, piedad.

She became a barmaid just out of menarche,
       fanning herself with a conch.
          It's useless to question the sea.

Who's to say the burrow where the grackle laid
       its pearls couldn't have been my bed?

Who's to say that when she loved she didn't learn
       to carve a dummy head to speak?

       but everyone listened.

A Mereology of Coyolxauhqui

•

I kept my chipped heart
        sistered
                to the bone.

Rattled when I was rattled,
                razored when I was razored,
        decomposed.

        The eye looked inward
but the mouth was closed.
                I missed things.

Then I opened my mouth
        and looked out,
                but misremembered
                        the things I had learned.

        There was grief in that shallow
                but I couldn't dig it out.

I posed my echoing body
        in *totentanz,* mouth
                closed.

••

This is the arm used for beating,
                mixing paint, drinking Carta Blanca,
fucking.

This is the hand used to salute
        the good old boys and ranchers,
                rinches and bloodletters.

        These are the fingers
scattered on the zocalo
                miming a recluse.

These are the nails worn brown
                by a chattering mouth
about to lose its house.

This is the bed where the shrunken
        heart disassembles itself,
attempting to drown.

•••

I was a little girl again.
I was a little boy again.
I was the thief who burned down
the cost-effective warehouse.
I was the slave who blamed the fire
on sinister spics.
I was the girl who claimed
the Toltec boy had hitched up my skirt.
I was the boy who claimed the girl
hid a heart under her tattered shirt.
I was the servant who admonished
the workers who lashed their children that night.
I was the Lord of the Moon.
I was the son who pressured the Lord
to bring back a trophy wetback.
I was the blade that made the boy
into a man.

I was the woman who fixed herself
into the blade.

••••

She plunged to the bottom
          of a blood sea.
          Her father told her,
                    You are a pink brittle star,
                    you must belong.
                              He lathered her body in chum.

His hands, her grandfather's hands,
          her brother's hands—
                    they were always attempting.
          She slept in a hammock
                    sewn from their pleadings.

After they were full, they ran
          to the nearest knoll
and evacuated her bones.

—

Since I am a mother
I take my medicine
on the floor, heart
in place of the head,
a bouquet of scrapes
and cuts.

Since I am a sister
I paint a red arrow
on my breasts, pointing
to the umbilical cord

where they rest their heads
and wait for the grief to collect.

Since I am a daughter
I hold my mother's head
in my hands, one on each ear
like a safe of corn.

I turn the head away
to face its influence,
warm my hands
in the makeshift womb.

•—

She speaks in the startled
                gestures of a mime, tumescent
        as she is, overworked
                with the nurses' hands
and their tireless resistance
to care.

        They give credit
to their defenses, the way
                they muffle the potted asters
                        in each room.
It is not a veneer.
                They bend and lift
        and strike, careless
                        as a hunter.

••—

For having doubted,
for the contortion,

for having breathed,
for having spoken,
for the yelp and the woof,
for having lived, in other words,
she is thrown ribbons of tissue
pickled in gray blood.

Her room is littered
like a wedding.

She is not given,
she is given away.

Her sin sits humbly
on the mortgaged hillock
of her tongue.

●●●—

        Three times a day
    they place a tab of ash on my lips.
             I wait for the wine, but cannot drink.
    Instead, my body feeds on air
        like an annelid.
           I taste of remorse
in the room's clockwork,
      how it would rather be filled with glaciers
and crinkled rose hip.
          Do I say I would trowel out
      the doctor's Klein bottle heart
if I could form words with my own mouth?
             One less weapon in his arsenal.
          Do I say I would raze my own house
      if I could talk?

Baedeker for a Life Cut with Danger

(John Valadez, *Car Show*, 2001; oil on canvas)

I don't have night's number. Wouldn't know it
if I went through a phone book
with a highlighter and a bloodhound.

Where's it hidden in her halter top,
the Aztec tats he plays loud as tom-toms
every time he takes his T-shirt off?

I worry about the sun in this backyard
barbecue. What if they added wrong,
and it's heavy enough to go black hole?

There go my tax returns. There goes the bread
I baked in the shape of a rosary.

Better to sing a war ballad. When I was a kid
all I wanted was to nurse a bloody rifle
between my thighs. I could've galloped
with Villa, a flask of pulque slung across my waist.

But don't mistake me for a sympathizer.
I hoard rejection in my cheeks
and porcupine needles for your outreach.
During the day, I'm a strain on group
identity. Rolling twenties in a street

lined with palms, samuraied by Hurricane Dolly.
Pouring myself into a junked Impala
with the winos from the VFW.

I know a little Spanish, the bristly kind
you speak when you want a Granny Smith
at the grocer. The tongue throws off

its crutches. You've got to think in a deeper
hunger so a round brown stomach can carry
your swollen arguments. So what are you?
And there is silence.

Notice how nothing that matters has a mouth.

Rodney Gomez lives in Brownsville, Texas, and works as an urban planner. He holds a bachelor's degree from Yale and an M.F.A. in creative writing from the University of Texas–Pan American. His poems have appeared in various literary journals and anthologies, including *Denver Quarterly, Devil's Lake, Fourteen Hills, Barrow Street, Nimrod,* and *Salt Hill.* He received the Editors' Prize from *RHINO* in 2013 and has held residencies at the Atlantic Center for the Arts and the Santa Fe Art Institute. He also served on the board of Migrant Health Promotion, a nonprofit organization dedicated to improving the health and well-being of migrants, immigrants, and related populations.